INFORMATION
EXPLORER
JUNIOR

Get to the Right Site

by Ann Truesdell

CHERRY LAKE PUBLISHING · ANN ARBOR, MICHIGAN

A NOTE TO PARENTS AND TEACHERS: Please remind your children how to stay safe online before they do the activities in this book.

CHERRY LAKE
Publishing

A NOTE TO KIDS: Always remember your safety comes first!

Published in the United States of America
by Cherry Lake Publishing
Ann Arbor, Michigan
www.cherrylakepublishing.com

Content Adviser: Gail Dickinson, PhD, Associate Professor, Old Dominion University

Book design and illustration: The Design Lab

Photo credits: Cover, ©Szasz-Fabian Ilka Erika/Shutterstock, Inc.; page 10, ©Cuky/Dreamstime.com; page 11, ©Enrico Battilana/Dreamstime.com; page 15, ©samotrebizan/Shutterstock, Inc.; page 19, ©iStockphoto.com/quavondo

Library of Congress Cataloging-in-Publication Data
Truesdell, Ann.
  Get to the right site / by Ann Truesdell.
    p. cm.—(Information explorer junior)
  Includes bibliographical references and index.
  ISBN 978-1-61080-365-6 (lib. bdg.)—ISBN 978-1-61080-374-8 (e-book)—ISBN 978-1-61080-390-8 (pbk.)
1. Computer network resources—Evaluation—Juvenile literature. 2. Internet searching—Juvenile literature. I. Title.
  ZA4201.T77 2012
  025.042'5—dc23   2011034505

Cherry Lake Publishing would like to acknowledge
the work of The Partnership for 21st Century Skills.
Please visit *www.21stcenturyskills.org* for more information.

Printed in the United States of America
Corporate Graphics Inc.
January 2012
CLSP10

Table of Contents

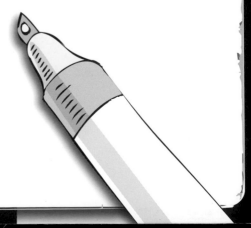

CHAPTER ONE

Online Adventures

"Everyone needs to do a report for homework," says your teacher. "Go **online** and find out about Christopher Columbus. Use your computer to search the **Internet**." This assignment sounds like fun! You have looked for information in books before. Now you will practice using the Internet to find information.

The Internet is an excellent source of free information. There are **Web sites** on almost every topic you can think of.

The Internet is packed with information about almost any topic you can imagine.

4

You can use computers to do many different things.

Many Web sites offer video and audio along with text and pictures, plus links to other Web sites with even more information.

However, you must be careful when you do **research** on the Internet. It's not the same as using a book. Nonfiction books are usually written by experts on a topic. Publishers double check that the information written is correct. The Internet is different. Anybody can post information on the Internet, but not everyone posts information that is correct. Plus, there is so much information on the Internet that it can be tricky to find the right site for you. Read on to learn how to find the best Web site for your research needs!

To get a copy of this activity, visit www.cherrylakepublishing.com/activities.

Activity

Books and the Internet are two very different resources, but one is not better than the other. You will choose when to use the Internet versus a book depending on what you are looking for and what options you have.

See if you can figure out which resource would be better for you to use in the situations below.

1. Your teacher says to find an article on a current event.
2. You want to find out more about your favorite TV show.
3. You need information about an animal for a research report and you want to make sure that the information is true.
4. You would like to watch a video to learn more about a topic.

ANSWERS:
1. The **Internet** changes every second. New articles and Web sites are always being posted. This makes the Internet a great resource for current events!
2. The **Internet** is a great resource for topics that might not have a book written about them, such as TV shows.
3. **Books** are more likely to be written by an expert than Web sites. The facts in books are also double-checked by the publisher. You have to be careful when you use a Web site for information. You have to decide if the site looks reliable on your own.
4. The **Internet** has many Web sites that feature videos to help you learn about a topic.

CHAPTER TWO

Start Your Engines!

It's time to do your online research about Christopher Columbus. Start by using a **search engine**. A search engine is a computer program that helps you find words or information. You type in words you are searching for. A search engine looks on the Internet. It works to find matches for those words. The matches, or results, are called Web sites.

Choose the search engine you like best.

There are search engines for doing all kinds of research. Some good search engines for kids are:

- *www.boolify.org*
- *www.kidrex.org*
- *http://kids.yahoo.com*
- *http://kidsclick.org*
- *www.askkids.com*

You will get a lot of results when you search for popular topics.

Suppose you begin your search by carefully typing in "Columbus." (It's important to spell your search words correctly.) Your search will probably turn up millions of results! The sites will not only be about Christopher Columbus. Cities that are named Columbus will show up, too. You'll even get sites about Columbus Day!

You will have to narrow your search. You only want information about the explorer Christopher Columbus. This time, type in "Christopher Columbus." A list of thousands of new sites will pop up. But now they're only about Columbus himself. Each site listed will have a brief **description** of itself.

Now it's time to do some clever detective work. You can do different searches to find different information about Christopher Columbus. Let's find the right sites for your report!

You need to enter the right search terms to find information about Christopher Columbus.

Activity

What if you change your search words a little? You will get different search results. Let's search for three slightly different subjects.

1. Take out your pencil and notebook. Use a ruler to draw three long lines down one page.

2. Write "Christopher Columbus report" at the top of the first column. Write "Christopher Columbus voyages" at the top of the second column. Write "Christopher Columbus explorer" at the top of the third column.

3. Do an Internet search for each of those three subjects. Look at the results of each search. Write down the first three sites that come up in each search.

Do you notice any differences in each search? What other search words could you have used?

Christopher Columbus report	Christopher Columbus voyages	Christopher Columbus explorer

CHAPTER THREE

Ask the Right Questions

Look at the different sites on your list. Read the brief descriptions. You want to find the most helpful sites. Ask yourself these questions:

- **"Is the site written for someone my age?"**
  You want to understand what is written. Then the site will be **valuable** to you. Can't understand it? Then the site is probably meant for older students.

Christopher Columbus Biography

Christopher Columbus Awards ★ Innovation Generation ★ Middle School Students ... Once several ideas have been suggested, begin a more in-depth discussion ...

This site tells you who the site is written for.

Only trust information that comes from reliable sources.

- **"Who wrote the information?"**

  Most **reliable** Web sites tell you who wrote the information. Is the author an **authority** on the subject? Search the author's name on the Internet. You can learn more about his or her **qualifications**. Sometimes organizations are related to the subject. Their Web sites will often have the best information.

- **"Is the information correct?"**

  Let's say one site says that Columbus was from Russia. Stop right there! Visit a few other sites. Learn where *they* say Columbus was born. Look at an encyclopedia or a book. The information should all be the same. That first site was the only one to mention Russia. So you know you can't trust that site.

- **"Is the information current?"**

  A Web site often tells you when it was last **updated**. Information changes over time. Facts about Columbus are found at history sites. History sites should be updated every 5 years.

- **"Does the site list other references?"**

  The author got information from references. References are books, articles, or other Web sites. Most good Web sites will list those references.

Activity

Test your skills as a Web site detective. Find a site about your favorite animal. Read an article at that site. What is the name of the author? Is that person an authority on the animal? How would you find out? Does the site say when it was last updated? Does the site list other references? Let's say you have to write a report on this animal. Would you use this site to do your research? Why or why not?

CHAPTER FOUR

Is It the Right Site?

You're ready to decide which sites to use for your research. Sometimes a site looks great. But maybe not all your questions were answered. That site might not be not complete. It might be a poor choice for your research.

Sometimes, a Web site can be misleading. It might have been updated this year. But it still contains information that is wrong. You should find better choices.

Christopher Columbus

Christopher Columbus: Explorer.
Christopher Columbus (1751–1806) was an Italian explorer who realized that the world was round and sailed across the . . .

Can you tell what is wrong with this web site link?

18

You'll be an online research expert in no time!

Think about all the questions you asked. Make sure the site meets your needs. One site may not answer all your research questions. Then you'll need more than one site. That will give you the best information for your report.

You will have to do online research more and more. Use the tools you learned here every time. You'll soon become an authority at finding the best sites.

Activity

Smart detectives take notes. So do smart researchers! Take notes about the Web sites you visit. Get out a sheet of paper. Make a checklist like the one on the opposite page. Think about each site. Answer each question. Does this information make you want to use the Web site?

Now put it all together. Will you use any of the sites? Why or why not?

To get a copy of this activity, visit www.cherrylakepublishing.com/activities.

Questions to Ask	Yes? No?	Use the Site	Don't Use the Site
Is the Web site about your topic?			
Is the Web site easy for you to read and understand?			
Do the facts seem to be correct?			
Is the writer an authority on the topic?			

Glossary

authority (uh-THOR-uh-tee) someone who is skilled or knows a lot about a subject

description (dee-SKRIP-shuhn) words or sentences that tell about something

Internet (IN-tur-net) the electronic network that allows millions of computers around the world to connect together

online (on-LINE) connected to other computers through the Internet

qualifications (kwa-luh-fuh-KAY-shunz) skills or abilities that make someone able to do a job or task

references (REH-frunts-iz) books, Web sites, magazines, or other types of works used to find information

reliable (ri-LYE-uh-buhl) trustworthy or dependable

research (REE-surch) to look for information on a topic

search engine (SURCH EN-juhn) a computer program that helps you find words or information you request

updated (UP-day-tid) changed something, such as a Web site, in order to include the latest information

valuable (VAL-yuh-buhl) important in some way, such as important information

Web sites (WEB SITES) connected groups of pages on the Internet, usually about a single topic or several closely related topics

Find Out More

BOOKS

Jakubiak, David J. *A Smart Kid's Guide to Doing Internet Research*. New York: PowerKids Press, 2010.

Oxlade, Chris. *My First Internet Guide*. Chicago: Heinemann Educational Books, 2007.

WEB SITES

Boston Public Library

www.bpl.org/KIDS/Evaluate.htm
www.bpl.org/KIDS/Glossary.htm

Check out these sites to learn how to use the Internet for school reports. The easy-to-use glossary of computer words and terms is worth visiting.

Index

About the Author

Ann Truesdell is a school library media specialist and teacher in Michigan. She and her husband, Mike, love traveling and spending time with their children, James and Charlotte.